Thanks to Marie-Dominique de Teneuille,
Béatrice Foulon, Frédérique Kartouby,
Hugues Charreyron and Annick Duboscq.

for Vianney and Flamine,

Translation
Isabel Ollivier
Design and layout
Chloé Bureau du Colombier
Photoengraving
Haudressy
Printed by
Imprimerie Alençonnaise

Cover illustration:
a detail from *The Rape of Helen* by Guido Reni

Violaine Bouvet-Lanselle
Marie Sellier

My Little Louvre

Réunion
des Musées
Nationaux

At the Louvre, *there is* a glass pyramid so clear
that you can see the skies of Paris above.
At the Louvre, *there is* the palace of the French kings
stretching out its arms to invite you in.

At the Louvre, *there are* fountains murmuring:

"Come and see the treasures of the biggest museum in the world."

Inside the Louvre, *there are* colours, *there is* marble and gold,

there are paintings, heroes, knick-knacks, and...

there are ... demons

I am the demon Pazuzu,

the king of evil spirits.

I play hide-and-seek with the winds,

I fly and whirl about,

grimacing to make people sick.

But I can also be very kind.

You just have to ask me politely

and give me a present or two.

Mesopotamia
The Demon Pazuzu
about 900 BC

there are ... happy dead people

We look alive and yet we are dead.

We are man and wife.

We didn't want to be separated

so we were put in the same tomb.

Here we are on our couch,

all brushed and dressed up,

ready for lunch.

Etruria
Sarcophagus of the Married Couple
about 520-510 BC

there are... warriors in long skirts

We are archers
in the army of Darius.
Our king is powerful,
our bows are very long
and our arrows are sharp.
We are proud of our victory,
so we are marching in single file
along the walls of his palace.
We are wearing our ceremonial robes
and we are made of baked brick.

Mesopotamia
Frieze of Archers (Palace of Darius)
about 500 BC

13

there is... a bird woman

I have wings like a bird,

but I lost my head and my arms

when I fell off the high rock

I used to perch on.

The sea and the wind

were my friends,

in those days.

In the Louvre,

they have put me

at the top of some stairs

where I sometimes get bored.

Greece
The Victory of Samothrace
about 199 BC

there is... a man with crystal eyes

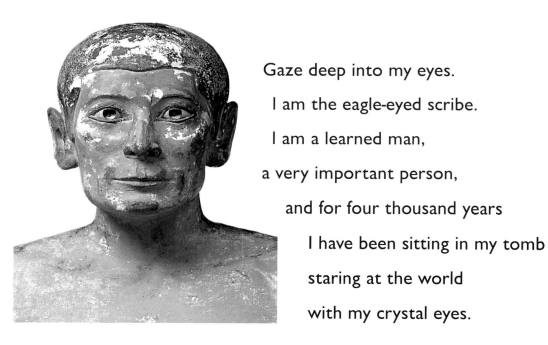

Gaze deep into my eyes.
  I am the eagle-eyed scribe.
  I am a learned man,
a very important person,
  and for four thousand years
    I have been sitting in my tomb
    staring at the world
    with my crystal eyes.

Egypt
Seated Scribe
about 2600-2350 BC

there are ... boxes inside boxes

What is inside that big box?

A smaller box.

And what is in the second box?

An even smaller box.

And in the third box?

A girl wound up in bandages.

Her name is Tamutnefret.

The day she died

her father was so sad

that he wanted to protect

her lovely body

in the world of the dead.

19

there are ... the treasures of the Kings of France

I'm the new King of France!

I had to go from Paris to Rheims

to be crowned. On the way,

I rode through Saint Denis

and picked up the royal treasures:

the glorious sword,

the golden sceptre

and the precious crown.

Everything I needed

to be crowned

King of France.

France,
18th century
Crown of Louis XV
1722

21

there is... a murderer

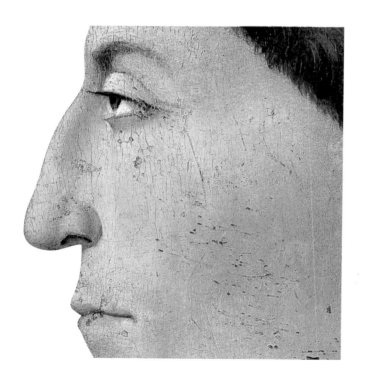

I am a cruel warlord,

a fearsome enemy.

Everyone hates me

and that suits me fine!

I killed my wife,

because she annoyed me so!

I'm very pleased

with my portrait:

I look as cold and sharp

as my sword blade.

Piero della Francesca
Portrait
of Sigismond
Malatesta
about 1430

there are ... two sisters in a bath tub

Look how pretty
my sister Gabrielle is!
She has golden hair
and very white skin!
She is so pretty
that King Henry
liked her best of all.
I am pinching her nipple
to tell you that she and the king
had a baby prince. They called him Cesar.

Fontainebleau School
Gabrielle d'Estrées and One of Her Sisters
about 1594

25

there is... a very ugly nose

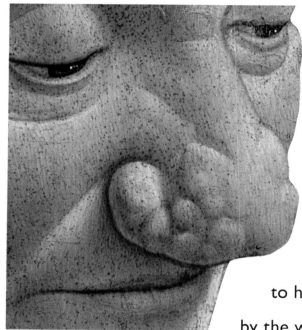

What a nose!
It is enormous, bumpy, and swollen.
Just like a big potato,
or a mountain
bursting with buds in spring.
But the little boy
doesn't mind.
He is listening
to his grandfather telling stories
by the wide-open window.

26

Ghirlandajo
Old Man and his Grandson
about 1490

there is... the Sun King

I am Louis XIV!

The Château of Versailles was built for me!

I am Louis XIV!

The handsomest, the greatest,

the most powerful king of all time!

I had this portrait painted for my grandson.

But it is much too splendid for him.

I shall keep it myself.

After all,

I am Louis XIV!

Hyacinthe Rigaud
Portrait of Louis XIV
1701

there is... a lion having a feast!

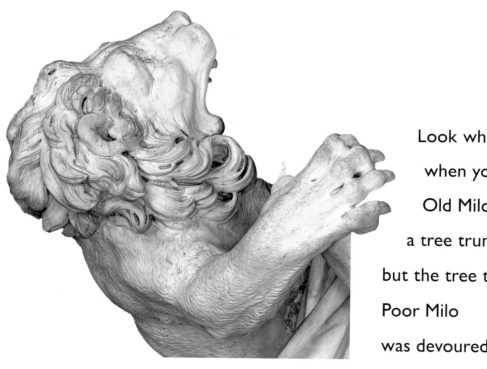

Look what happens
when you try to be too clever.
Old Milo wanted to split
a tree trunk with his bare hands
but the tree trapped his fingers.
Poor Milo
was devoured by a lion!

Pierre Puget
Milo of Crotona
1670-1683

there is... a strong-armed dentist

" Come on, just relax,

   you won't feel a thing! "

      But, the tooth-drawer is a liar.

      It hurts horribly!

      The poor man

      is bellowing with pain.

      The moral of the story is:

      if you don't want

      your teeth to rot,

      brush them!

Gérard Dou
The Tooth-Drawer
1647

there is... a family breakfast

"Breakfast is ready, come and drink
your chocolate," says Mummy.
But I would rather play
with my horse and my doll.
Daddy, who is an artist,
says there won't be any left,
because my sister will eat it all up.
But I don't care. I know him!
All he wants to do is paint.
As soon as he has finished
his breakfast he will go back
to his studio and put us all in a painting.

François Boucher
Breakfast
1739

there is... a pack of cheats

Keep your eyes open, you ninny!
Look what those three rascals
are telling each other with their hands
and their sly looks. Look up, quickly,
and you will see the crafty fellow
slipping the ace of diamonds
out of his belt. It's the winning card!
Look sharp, you ninny,
or you'll be fleeced!

Georges de La Tour
The Card Sharp with the Ace of Diamonds
about 1630

there is... a slimy fish

"Yuck! Revolting.

Pooh! Repulsive!

Ooooh!" says the cat, with a shiver.

"Look at the stingray...

It's disgusting,

it looks as though it is laughing!

I turn my head away

but my eyes swivel round.

I can't drag myself away.

It attracts me

and repulses me."

Jean-Baptiste-Siméon Chardin
The Rayfish
1725

there is ... Little Red Riding Hood

"Yum, yum.

I'll gobble her up!"

mutters the wolf, licking his chops.

"A tasty morsel!

Her granny was a bit tough.

She will be just right for dessert."

You should look behind you,

Little Red Riding Hood!

If you saw your granny's dress,

you would run away fast!

François-Richard Fleury
Little Red Riding Hood
about 1840

there is... Mona Lisa, of course!

Mona Lisa is so well known

that sometimes it is a little disappointing to see her.

The painting is so dark, and so small!

Why does everyone like her so much?

Because of her hands,

folded one over the other?

Or her smile? Or her eyes

that follow me around?

She has bewitched me,

I don't want to leave her.

Leonardo da Vinci
Mona Lisa
about 1501-1506

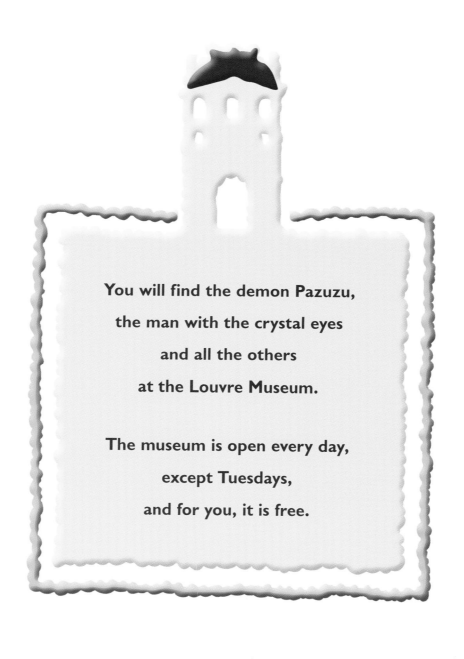

You will find the demon Pazuzu,

the man with the crystal eyes

and all the others

at the Louvre Museum.

The museum is open every day,

except Tuesdays,

and for you, it is free.

Photos:

Réunion des musées nationaux

Photos by D. Arnaudet, G. Blot,

H. Chuzeville, C. Jean, Ch. Larrieu,

H. Lewandowski, R. G. Ojeda, J. Schormans.

Registered: December 2001

ISBN 2-7118-4423-4

JC 20 4423

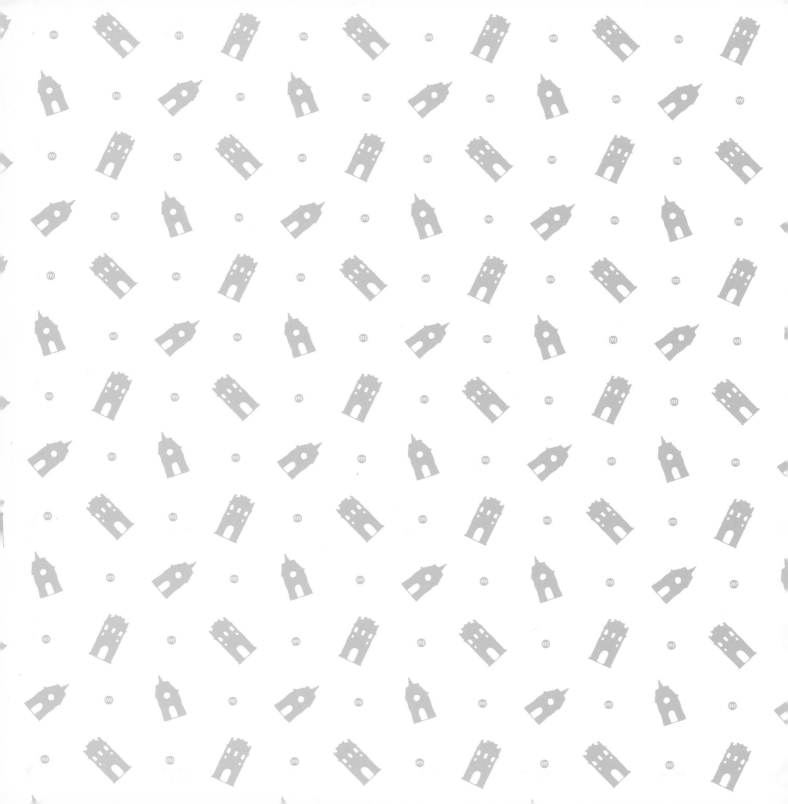